Edible Wild Plants Foraging

From Nature's Bounty to Your Plate: Recipes and Revelations

John Walsh

Table of the Contents:

Introduction

The Ancient Art of Foraging: A Brief History of Wild Food Hunting.

Long before supermarkets lined their aisles with neatly packaged vegetables and gleaming fruits, our ancestors roamed the wild landscapes, seeking nourishment from the earth. This primal pursuit, known as foraging, was not just an activity; it was a way of life, a dance with nature, and a testament to the symbiotic relationship between humans and their environment.

Foraging, in its essence, is the act of gathering wild food from natural environments. This could be anything from plucking berries off bushes to digging up roots from beneath the moist forest floor. Our early ancestors, with intimate knowledge of their surroundings, could decipher which plants were nutritious, which were medicinal, and which were potentially deadly. This knowledge was often passed down through generations, solidifying the cultural and survival significance of foraging.

As civilizations grew, we began to move away from the nomadic lifestyle. The advent of agriculture meant that communities could settle in one place, cultivating the land to produce food. Over time, the art of foraging took a backseat, becoming less of a necessity and more of a specialized skill or hobby.

However, as modern society grapples with issues of sustainability, health, and reconnecting with nature, there is a renewed interest in this ancient practice. Today, enthusiasts venture into forests, meadows, and even urban landscapes, searching for edible wild plants not only to feed their bodies but also to nourish their souls.

This book aims to reintroduce the reader to the world of edible wild plants, taking you on a journey from the origins of foraging to its contemporary resurgence. Along the way, you will discover the beauty of wild foods, learn the skills needed to safely harvest them, and explore recipes to bring these natural ingredients to your table.

Why Forage Today: Health and Environmental Benefits

In an age of convenience, where most of our food comes pre-packaged and often from thousands of miles away, the idea of foraging might seem archaic, even unnecessary. However, the resurgence in foraging's popularity in recent years isn't just a nod to our ancestral roots; it's a response to the growing understanding of its manifold benefits, both for our health and the environment. This chapter delves into why foraging is more relevant today than ever before.

1. Nutritional Bounty: The Health Benefits of Wild Foods

Wild plants often offer a richer nutritional profile compared to their cultivated counterparts. Their struggle for survival in the wild, facing pests, competition, and variable weather, equips them with a diverse array of vitamins, minerals, and antioxidants.

- **Rich in Antioxidants:** Many wild plants have evolved to produce compounds that protect them from UV radiation, pests, and diseases. When consumed, these compounds, like flavonoids and polyphenols, offer us protection against oxidative stress.

- **Diverse Micronutrients:** From nettles rich in iron to dandelions loaded with vitamin K, wild foods can be a source of essential vitamins and minerals often missing from modern diets.

2. Zero Carbon Footprint Food

With concerns over the carbon footprint of the foods we consume, foraging offers a sustainable alternative. Foraged foods require no transportation, no packaging, and no agricultural inputs like pesticides or fertilizers, making them one of the most eco-friendly food sources available.

3. Reconnecting with Nature

The act of foraging is meditative. It requires patience, observation, and a deep connection with the land. This bond with nature has profound psychological benefits, including reduced stress, improved mood, and enhanced mindfulness.

4. Promoting Biodiversity

Foraging fosters a deep appreciation for diverse ecosystems. As more people understand the value of wild foods, there's a growing incentive to protect these natural habitats from deforestation, pollution, and urban sprawl.

5. A Solution to Overfarming and Soil Depletion

Relying solely on agriculture has its downsides. Intense farming practices can lead to soil depletion, loss of arable land, and a decline in crop nutritional value. Wild foods, on the other hand, grow in harmony with their environment, promoting soil health and ecological balance.

6. Building Community

Foraging is often a communal activity. Whether joining local foraging groups or sharing the day's harvest with family and friends, it fosters a sense of community, encouraging people to share knowledge, resources, and experiences.

Understanding Your Environment

The art of foraging is deeply rooted in understanding and adapting to one's environment. At the heart of this is recognizing the influence of climate and the changing seasons on the availability and variety of wild foods. This chapter will guide you through the different climatic zones and the significance of seasons in the realm of foraging.

1. Climatic Zones: The World's Natural Pantry

The Earth's surface is divided into several climatic zones, each with its unique vegetation and wildlife. These zones determine not just the type of plants that grow but also their nutritional content, adaptability, and life cycles.

- **Tropical Zones:** These regions, situated near the equator, experience warm temperatures year-round. Rainforests, savannas, and monsoon regions fall under this category. Expect a variety of fruits, nuts, and roots, like jackfruit, durian, or yams.
- **Subtropical Zones:** Characterized by hot summers and mild winters, these regions offer a diverse range of fruits like citrus, avocados, and olives.

- **Temperate Zones:** These zones experience distinct seasons with warm summers and cold winters. Berries, nuts, and various leafy greens are commonly found in these areas.

- **Cold Zones:** Encompassing the polar regions and high altitudes, the cold zones have a short growing season. While foraging options might be limited, you can find unique plants like cloudberries, lingonberries, and some hardy roots.

- **Arid and Semi-Arid Zones:** These are the world's deserts and dry regions. Plants here, such as cacti and certain succulents, have evolved to thrive with minimal water.

2. Seasons: Nature's Calendar

Understanding the seasons is paramount for a forager. Each season brings its unique bounty, and recognizing this can ensure a varied and nutritious harvest throughout the year.

- **Spring:** As the land awakens from winter, spring offers tender greens, shoots, and early berries. It's an excellent time for foraging plants like wild garlic, ramps, and young nettles.

- **Summer:** This is the season of abundance. Fruits, berries, flowers, and various herbs are at their peak. Look for blackberries, chamomile, and wild strawberries.
- **Autumn:** As the days start to shorten, trees and plants prepare for winter, offering a bounty of nuts, seeds, and late-season fruits. It's also the prime season for mushroom foraging.
- **Winter:** While it might seem barren, the winter landscape hides several edible treasures. Look for hardy greens, roots, and some late or early fungi.

3. The Interplay of Climate and Seasons

While climatic zones provide a broad understanding of regional vegetation, the seasons offer a timeline for harvesting. For a successful foraging experience, one must merge knowledge of both. For instance, while spring in a temperate zone might bring wild garlic, the same season in a tropical zone could offer fresh mango shoots.

Understanding your environment is the cornerstone of foraging. Recognizing the climatic zone and syncing with the rhythm of the seasons ensures not only a bountiful harvest but also a deep connection with the land. As you step into the world of foraging, let the climate and seasons be your guiding compass.

Common Habitats and Their Characteristic Plants

Foraging is as much about understanding the landscapes around us as it is about knowing individual plants. Every habitat, with its unique set of conditions, hosts specific plants adapted to thrive there. This chapter explores some common habitats and the plants you can expect to find in each.

1. Forests

Forests, be it temperate, tropical, or boreal, are treasure troves of biodiversity.

- **Temperate Forests:** These dense woodlands are filled with oaks, maples, and birches. Foragers can find wild garlic, morel mushrooms, blueberries, and ramps during different seasons.
- **Tropical Forests:** Lush and evergreen, these forests harbor plants like jackfruit, guava, durian, and a myriad of medicinal herbs and roots.

- **Boreal or Taiga Forests:** Dominated by conifers, these cold forests house cloudberries, lingonberries, and fungi like the chaga mushroom.

2. Meadows and Grasslands

These open habitats, kissed by sunlight, support a wide variety of grasses, flowers, and herbs.

- **Characteristic Plants:** Wildflowers like chamomile, dandelion, and clover are common. Edible grasses and sedges also thrive here, and during certain times of the year, mushrooms like field mushrooms might appear.

3. Wetlands (Marshes, Bogs, and Swamps)

These waterlogged lands are rich in biodiversity, and while they can be tricky to navigate, they offer a unique foraging experience.

- **Characteristic Plants:** Cattails, wild rice, and cranberries are some of the edible plants one can find. The spongy grounds of bogs might also give rise to cloudberries and other bog-specific berries.

4. Coastal and Beach Areas

The interface of land and sea, these regions have plants adapted to salty and often sandy conditions.

- **Characteristic Plants:** Sea vegetables like seaweed (kelp, nori, dulse), samphire, and sea purslane are abundant. The occasional sea beet might also be spotted.

5. Mountainous and Alpine Regions

The rugged terrain and thinner air of these regions give rise to hardy plants, some of which offer unique flavors and medicinal properties.

- **Characteristic Plants:** Edible plants like wild thyme, sorrel, and certain tubers can be found. During the brief summer, alpine berries like bilberries might also make an appearance.

6. Deserts and Arid Regions

While harsh and seemingly inhospitable, deserts house a range of plants adapted to minimal water availability.

- **Characteristic Plants:** Cacti like the prickly pear, succulents like aloe vera, and hardy shrubs offering berries are typical finds in these regions.

Each habitat, with its unique characteristics, supports specific plants that have adapted over millennia to thrive there. As a forager, understanding these habitats is as crucial as knowing the plants themselves. Not only does it ensure a successful foraging expedition, but it also deepens our connection to the land, teaching us the intricate ways in which nature weaves its tapestry of life.

Getting Started with Foraging

Embarking on your foraging journey is an exciting venture, connecting you more deeply with the land and the myriad of plants it nurtures. However, the wild is a vast and varied place, and not every plant is friendly or edible. Prioritizing safety is paramount. This chapter establishes the golden rules to ensure a fruitful and safe foraging experience.

1. Know Before You Go

It's vital to arm yourself with knowledge. Invest in a good regional field guide that provides clear pictures and descriptions of local plants. Familiarize yourself with it before heading out.

2. When in Doubt, Leave it Out

If you're unsure about a plant's identity or edibility, it's best not to consume it. Many edible plants have toxic look-alikes. It's better to err on the side of caution.

3. Start Small

As a beginner, focus on a few easily identifiable and safe plants. Gradually expand your repertoire as you gain experience and confidence.

4. Observe Growth Patterns

Many plants absorb toxins or pollutants from their environment. Avoid foraging near roadsides, industrial areas, or places that might have been sprayed with pesticides.

5. Respect Nature's Balance

Foraging is about harmony. Always leave behind more than you take to ensure the plant population remains healthy and vibrant. As a general rule, never harvest more than a third of a patch.

6. Learn from the Locals

Engaging with local foraging communities or elders can provide invaluable knowledge. They can share insights about regional plants, harvesting techniques, and even preparation methods.

7. Avoid Contaminated Areas

Be wary of areas that might be polluted, such as spots near factories, railways, or agricultural lands that might use heavy pesticides. Plants in such areas can absorb harmful chemicals.

8. Be Prepared

Carry essentials like a map, compass, knife, containers for collecting plants, and first aid. Ensure you dress appropriately for the terrain and weather.

9. Document Your Findings

Maintain a foraging journal. Documenting the plants you find, their locations, and any effects after consumption can be both a learning tool and a safety measure.

10. Familiarize Yourself with Local Laws

In some regions, foraging might be restricted or prohibited to preserve the natural habitat or protect endangered species. Always ensure you're foraging legally.

Conclusion

Foraging is an enriching experience, bridging the gap between humans and nature. However, the wild demands respect and caution. By adhering to these golden rules, not only will you ensure your safety and the wellbeing of the environment, but you'll also pave the way for a fulfilling and sustainable foraging journey.

Essential Tools for the Modern Forager

Foraging is an ancient practice, but modern advancements have provided us with tools that make the process easier, more efficient, and safer. From the traditional knife to digital apps that aid plant identification, equipping oneself can greatly enhance the foraging experience. This chapter delves into the must-have tools for the contemporary forager.

1. Field Guidebook

- **Description:** A comprehensive guidebook, specific to your region, that provides detailed information on local plants, their edibility, and medicinal properties.
- **Utility:** Helps in accurate plant identification, understanding seasonal availability, and ensuring safety.

2. Foraging Knife

- **Description:** A sturdy, foldable knife designed to harvest plants without damaging them or their surrounding environment.
- **Utility:** Essential for cutting stems, digging up roots, or slicing mushrooms.

3. Durable Collection Bags and Baskets

- **Description:** Cloth bags, mesh sacks, or traditional baskets used for collecting and transporting foraged items.
- **Utility:** Allows for the safe transport of delicate items and ensures adequate ventilation, especially for mushrooms.

4. Smartphone with Foraging Apps

- **Description:** Digital apps designed to aid plant identification through pictures and detailed descriptions.
- **Utility:** Offers instant information in the field, provides GPS tagging for location tracking, and helps in logging personal foraging records.

5. Compact Magnifying Glass

- **Description:** A pocket-sized lens that allows for a closer inspection of plants, especially smaller features.
- **Utility:** Aids in distinguishing similar-looking plants and observing intricate details vital for accurate identification.

6. Gloves

- **Description:** Protective gloves made of durable material to safeguard hands against thorns, nettles, or potential allergens.
- **Utility:** Provides protection while handling unfamiliar plants or navigating challenging terrains.

7. Journal and Pen

- **Description:** A personal diary to record observations, locations, harvest times, and personal experiences.
- **Utility:** Helps track and reflect on your foraging journey, building a repository of knowledge over time.

8. Maps and Compass

- **Description:** Traditional navigation tools to understand and navigate through unfamiliar terrains.
- **Utility:** Ensures you remain oriented, especially in areas with poor cellular reception, and helps in revisiting productive foraging spots.

9. Ethical Foraging Guidelines

- **Description:** A set of principles, either self-imposed or provided by local foraging communities, that guide sustainable harvesting.
- **Utility:** Ensures that foraging practices are eco-friendly and that plant populations remain undisturbed for future generations.

10. Personal First Aid Kit

- **Description:** A compact collection of essential first aid items such as antiseptics, band-aids, tweezers, and allergy medication.
- **Utility:** Ensures quick medical attention in case of minor injuries or allergic reactions.

While intuition and experience play a significant role in foraging, equipping oneself with the right tools can make the process more rewarding and secure. The modern forager, straddling the worlds of ancient wisdom and contemporary technology, has the unique advantage of having the best of both realms at their fingertips.

Common Edible Wild Plants

Dandelion (Taraxacum officinale)

In many lawns and fields, you'll likely spot the familiar yellow petals of the dandelion. While often dismissed as a mere weed, this hardy perennial is, in fact, a treasure trove of nutritional and medicinal benefits. With its array of edible parts, from leaves to flowers and roots, the humble dandelion has much to offer to the forager.

Origins and Distribution

Native to Eurasia, the dandelion has now spread and naturalized in many parts of the world, including North America, South America, and Australia. It thrives in a variety of habitats, from well-tended lawns to neglected urban lots, making it accessible to virtually anyone interested in foraging.

Morphology

The dandelion plant features a rosette of oblong, toothed leaves, from which a singular, hollow stalk arises, topped with a bright yellow flower. This bloom later matures into the iconic, globe-like seed head that children delight in blowing into the wind. The plant's deep taproot is dark brown on the outside but reveals a creamy white flesh inside.

Nutritional and Medicinal Benefits

Rich in vitamins A, C, and K, dandelion leaves are also a good source of calcium, potassium, iron, and magnesium. Beyond its nutritional profile, the plant has long been used in traditional medicine for its purported diuretic, anti-inflammatory, and liver-detoxifying properties.

Foraging and Harvesting

1. **Leaves:** Young leaves, harvested before the plant flowers, are the most tender and least bitter. They can be hand-picked from the base of the plant.
2. **Flowers:** Plucked just below the flower head, these can be collected anytime they are in bloom.
3. **Roots:** Best harvested in late fall or early spring, using a sturdy knife or small shovel, taking care to extract the entire root.

Culinary Uses

- **Salads:** Young leaves add a slightly bitter note to salads, somewhat akin to arugula. They can be mixed with other greens or used on their own.
- **Tea:** Both dried leaves and roots can be used to brew a nutritious herbal tea. The roots, when roasted, lend a flavor reminiscent of coffee.
- **Wine:** The bright yellow petals are a primary ingredient in traditional dandelion wine, producing a unique, sunny beverage perfect for summer.

Preparation Tips

- Wash the leaves thoroughly to remove any dirt or tiny insects.
- Blanching the leaves can help reduce their bitterness.
- The white sap or "milk" from the dandelion stem can be slightly bitter and is often avoided in culinary preparations.

Conclusion

The dandelion, often overlooked and underappreciated, is a testament to nature's generosity. As a symbol of resilience and adaptability, it offers a wealth of nutrients and flavors for those willing to see beyond its reputation as a simple weed. Next time you spot a patch of dandelions, consider the culinary and medicinal possibilities lying at your feet.

Nettles (Urtica dioica)

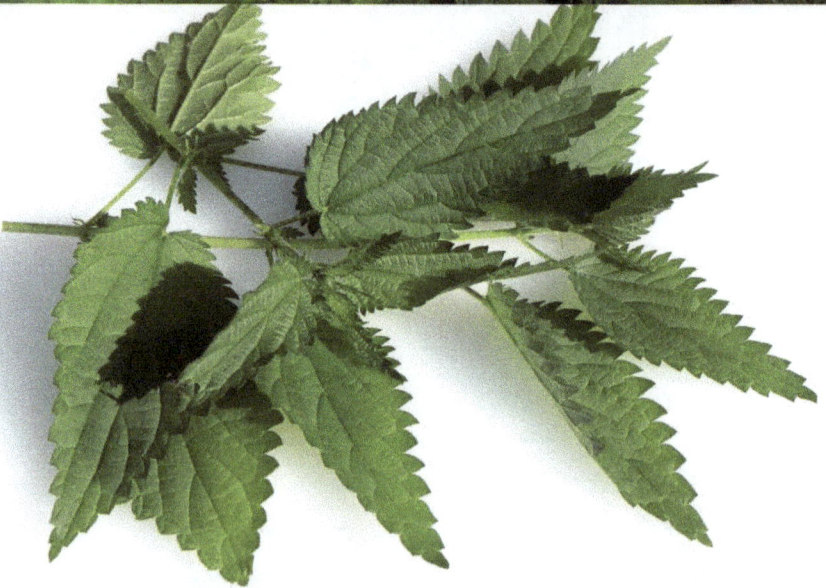

The stinging nettle, with its formidable reputation for causing temporary discomfort to the touch, may not be the first plant one thinks of consuming. However, for centuries, nettles have been a cornerstone in the diets and medicinal cabinets of various cultures, cherished for their myriad benefits and robust flavor.

Origins and Distribution

Nettles are native to Europe, Asia, northern Africa, and North America. They flourish in temperate regions and are often found in nitrogen-rich soils near water sources, forest edges, or human habitations. Their ubiquity in various environments makes them a common plant for foragers to encounter.

Morphology

Nettles can grow up to four feet in height and are recognized by their dark green, serrated, heart-shaped leaves with pointed tips. The entire plant, especially the undersides of the leaves and the stems, is covered in tiny, hair-like structures. These "hairs" contain a stinging substance, which can cause a burning sensation upon contact with skin.

Nutritional and Medicinal Benefits

Nettles are a powerhouse of nutrition. They are rich in vitamins A, C, and K, and also contain significant amounts of iron, calcium, magnesium, and protein. From a medicinal standpoint, nettles have been used to treat ailments like arthritis, allergies, and skin disorders. They are also considered diuretic and anti-inflammatory.

Foraging and Harvesting

1. **Young Leaves:** These are the primary edible part of the nettle plant. It's crucial to forage for them in the spring, before the plant flowers, as older leaves can develop gritty particles that might be irritating when ingested. Wearing gloves is essential to avoid getting stung.

Culinary Uses

- **Soups:** Perhaps the most famous dish is the classic nettle soup, where the young leaves are boiled and then blended with ingredients like potatoes, onions, and broth to create a creamy, green soup.

- **Teas:** Dried or fresh nettle leaves can be steeped in hot water to produce a mineral-rich tea with a pleasant, earthy taste.

- **Pesto:** Nettles can serve as a substitute for basil in pesto recipes. Blending them with garlic, pine nuts, parmesan cheese, and olive oil produces a rich and flavorful sauce perfect for pasta or as a spread.

Preparation Tips

- Always cook nettles before consumption. The heat neutralizes the stinging compounds, rendering the plant safe and pleasant to eat.

- When handling fresh nettles, it's advisable to wear gloves or use tongs to avoid contact with the stinging hairs.

- Blanching nettles in boiling water for a few minutes is a common first step in many recipes, as it softens the leaves and eliminates their sting.

Conclusion

The stinging nettle, once tamed by the heat of the kitchen, transforms from a feared weed into a culinary delight. It stands as a lesson in nature's paradoxes, where something seemingly adversarial can, with a bit of knowledge and care, become a nourishing ally. Embracing nettles is a nod to ancient culinary traditions and a testament to the adage that nature provides – if only we know where and how to look.

Wood Sorrel (Oxalis spp.)

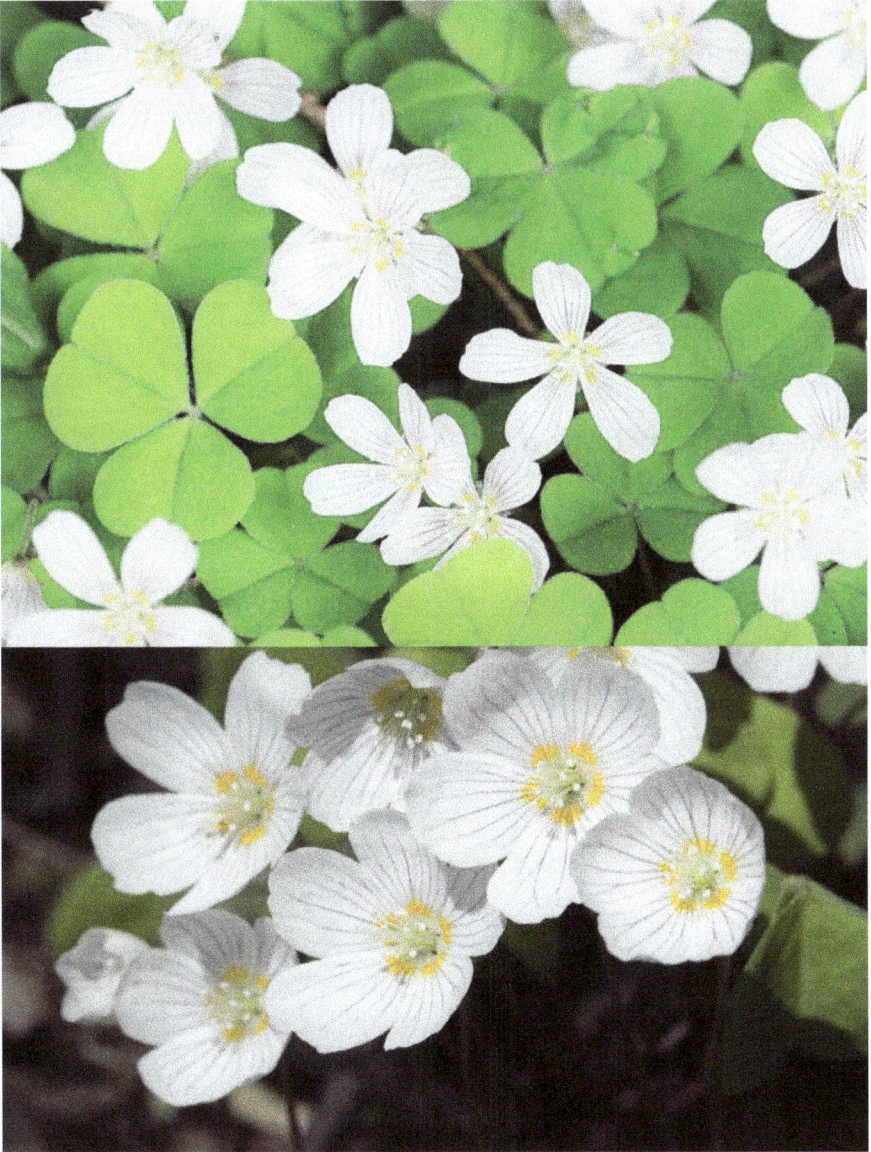

Brightening up many a woodland floor or shaded garden with its trifoliate, clover-like leaves and delicate flowers, wood sorrel is an enchanting find for the discerning forager. It's not only a feast for the eyes but offers a tantalizing tartness reminiscent of lemons. Its genus name, Oxalis, is derived from the Greek word for "sour," aptly describing the plant's taste profile.

Origins and Distribution

Wood sorrel belongs to the Oxalidaceae family and is widespread throughout most of the world, from North America to Europe, Asia, and Africa. Depending on the region and specific species, the plant may vary slightly in appearance, but its characteristic heart-shaped, trifoliate leaves are a common identifier.

Morphology

Most species of wood sorrel possess thin, delicate stems rising from a central point, with sets of three heart-shaped leaves, often mistaken for clover. The flowers, which bloom in various shades from white and yellow to pink or purple, are typically composed of five petals. Following the flowering stage, the plant produces fruit capsules filled with tiny seeds.

Nutritional and Medicinal Benefits

Wood sorrel contains a good amount of vitamin C, which contributed to its historical use in preventing scurvy among sailors. The plant also contains oxalic acid, which gives it its sour taste, but also means it should be consumed in moderation, especially by those with kidney conditions or prone to kidney stones.

Foraging and Harvesting

1. **Leaves:** These can be harvested throughout the growing season but are most tender during the spring. They should be plucked gently to ensure the plant continues to thrive.
2. **Flowers:** Best picked when fully open, typically during midday when they're most vibrant.
3. **Seeds:** Harvested when the fruit capsules mature and turn brown. They can be eaten directly or saved to grow new plants.

Culinary Uses

- **Salads:** The tart leaves and flowers can be sprinkled into salads, providing a refreshing lemony kick.
- **Garnishes:** Both the flowers and leaves serve as a beautiful and flavorful garnish for various dishes, from soups to desserts.
- **Lemony Flavoring:** The leaves can be infused in cold water to make a refreshing drink or added to dishes requiring a hint of tartness.

Preparation Tips

- Wood sorrel leaves are best consumed fresh to enjoy their full flavor. However, they can also be dried for later use in teas.
- Given the presence of oxalic acid, it's advisable to consume wood sorrel in moderation.
- Always ensure correct identification, as wood sorrel can be mistaken for clover or other plants.

Conclusion

Wood sorrel's allure lies not just in its delicate beauty but in its capacity to surprise the palate with its unexpected zest. For those who walk the woods or even the shaded corners of their gardens, this plant offers culinary adventures anchored in the very essence of wild food foraging. As with all wild plants, respect for nature and responsible harvesting ensure that the joys of wood sorrel can be experienced by generations to come.

Plantain (Plantago major)

Plantain, often overshadowed by more vibrant flora, humbly carpets many of the world's paths, lawns, and fields. Yet, its unassuming presence belies a long history of culinary and medicinal use. From ancient remedies to modern kitchens, Plantago major offers a fusion of tradition and contemporary applications to the informed forager.

Origins and Distribution

Originating in Europe and Central Asia, plantain has since spread globally. It's a testimony to the plant's adaptability that one can find it from urban environments to untouched meadows. Though sometimes branded a "weed," its persistence and usefulness might argue for a more esteemed title.

Morphology

Plantain boasts broad, oval leaves that emerge in a rosette from the ground. Its leaves have pronounced parallel veins. From the center of this leafy base, a tall, thin spike arises, dotted with tiny flowers that eventually give way to seed pods.

Nutritional and Medicinal Benefits

Historically, plantain has been a go-to remedy for various skin conditions, from insect bites to burns. The leaves contain anti-inflammatory properties and have been used in poultices to relieve pain and prevent infections. Internally, the seeds, being a source of dietary fiber, aid digestion.

Foraging and Harvesting

1. **Leaves:** Young leaves, picked during spring or after a rainfall, are the most tender and suitable for culinary purposes. Older leaves, while more fibrous, are still excellent for medicinal uses.
2. **Seeds:** Harvested in late summer, the seeds can be collected by stripping them off the mature flower stalks.

Culinary Uses

- **Salads:** Young plantain leaves can be chopped and added to salads, providing a mild, earthy flavor.
- **Medicinal Poultices:** The crushed or chewed leaves can be applied directly to wounds, bites, or stings to reduce

inflammation and pain. They can also be steeped in hot water, strained, and the liquid applied to affected areas.

Preparation Tips

- Prior to using plantain in culinary dishes, it's advisable to wash the leaves thoroughly, given their ground-level growth.
- While young leaves can be consumed raw, older leaves benefit from cooking to reduce their toughness – they can be steamed or sautéed.
- When making a poultice, fresh leaves are most effective. Simply crushing or chewing them releases their medicinal compounds.

Conclusion

Plantain, in its quiet resilience, embodies the treasures often overlooked in our immediate environment. Far from being a simple weed, it is a link to ancestral knowledge and a testament to the potency of nature's offerings. For the forager, every plantain leaf turned over is not just food or medicine, but a story of our interwoven history with the botanical world.

Lamb's Quarters (Chenopodium album)

Unmistakably verdant and with an often dusty-looking surface, Lamb's Quarters is a wild edible that quietly asserts its presence in gardens, fields, and waste places. Known by several names, including goosefoot and wild spinach, this plant is a delightful discovery for any forager seeking nutrient-rich wild greens.

Origins and Distribution

Hailing from Europe, Lamb's Quarters has comfortably established itself in many parts of the world. Today, it's a common sight across North America, Asia, and other regions, thriving in disturbed soils, garden edges, and agricultural lands.

Morphology

The plant typically has diamond or lance-shaped leaves, with the younger ones often covered in a whitish, powdery coating. The arrangement gives the plant its 'goosefoot' moniker, due to the shape's resemblance to a bird's foot. As it matures, Chenopodium album produces vertical clusters of tiny greenish flowers, which eventually yield small, black seeds.

Nutritional and Medicinal Benefits

Rich in vitamins A, C, and K, as well as minerals like calcium and potassium, Lamb's Quarters is a nutrient powerhouse. Its young leaves, in particular, offer a spinach-like flavor and can be a significant source of dietary fiber, protein, and other essential nutrients.

Foraging and Harvesting

1. **Young Leaves:** Best harvested in spring and early summer, they are tender and ideal for a variety of culinary uses.
2. **Seeds:** By late summer and early autumn, the seeds are ready for collection. Though tiny, they're nutritious and can be ground into flour or used as a grain substitute.

Culinary Uses

- **Salads:** The tender young leaves can be added raw to salads, offering a slightly salty and spinach-like taste.
- **Steamed Greens:** Older leaves can be lightly steamed and served as a side dish, often seasoned with a touch of butter, garlic, or lemon.

Preparation Tips

- Before culinary use, it's good practice to rinse the leaves, removing any dirt or powdery residue.
- For a richer flavor, sauté the leaves with a mix of garlic, onions, and your preferred herbs.
- While the seeds can be consumed raw, toasting them slightly enhances their nutty flavor and makes them a crunchy salad topping.

Conclusion

Lamb's Quarters is a testament to nature's generosity, offering both flavor and nutrition from what many might mistakenly deem an inconspicuous weed. Embracing this plant is not just a nod to sustainable eating but a step into a world where every patch of green holds culinary promise. Through informed foraging and respectful harvesting, one can savor the bounties of Chenopodium album and appreciate its rightful place in our diets.

Chickweed (Stellaria media)

A star in the world of foraging, chickweed, with its delicate blossoms and verdant tendrils, graces many a garden and meadow. This petite, sprawling herb, while sometimes dismissed as a mere garden interloper, holds culinary and medicinal treasures that have been celebrated for generations.

Origins and Distribution

Originally native to Europe, chickweed has since spread its tendrils globally, flourishing in temperate regions of North America, Asia, and beyond. Its resilience and adaptability make it a common sight in gardens, fields, and even cracks in urban pavements.

Morphology

Stellaria media sports small, paired leaves along slender, green stems. The plant gets its name from the tiny, star-like white flowers that emerge, each with five deeply notched petals – giving the appearance of ten. The entire plant is soft and somewhat succulent in texture, making it a refreshing edible.

Nutritional and Medicinal Benefits

Rich in vitamins and minerals, chickweed offers a plethora of nutrients, including vitamin C, calcium, and magnesium. Historically, chickweed has been used for its anti-inflammatory properties, often applied topically to soothe rashes or skin irritations.

Foraging and Harvesting

1. **Aerial Parts:** From late winter to spring, the lush green aerial parts of the chickweed plant are at their prime for harvesting. Using scissors or pinching with fingers ensures a gentle harvest.

Culinary Uses

- **Salads:** The fresh, crisp texture of chickweed makes it a delightful addition to salads, lending a mild and slightly grassy flavor.
- **Pesto:** Chickweed's soft stems and leaves blend smoothly into a green pesto. Mixed with garlic, nuts, and olive oil, it offers a wild, nutritious spin on the classic sauce.

Preparation Tips

- It's essential to wash chickweed thoroughly before consumption, ensuring any dirt or tiny insects are removed.
- When preparing pesto, chickweed can be blended with traditional basil for a nuanced flavor or used on its own for a distinctive wild green taste.
- Chickweed pairs well with lemon, garlic, and even mild cheeses, offering flexibility in various dishes.

Conclusion

Chickweed's gentle demeanor in the wild belies its potent nutritional value and versatility in the kitchen. Reconnecting with such wild edibles is more than just a culinary journey; it's a homage to traditional foodways and an embrace of nature's abundant generosity. Stellaria media invites foragers to look closer, to find the wonders that lie underfoot, and to celebrate the intricate dance of nature and nourishment.

Purslane (Portulaca oleracea)

Purslane, with its succulent leaves and reddish stems, is more than just an attractive groundcover. This unassuming plant, often dismissed as a common weed, has ancient roots in culinary traditions spanning continents, and offers a unique blend of flavors and health benefits.

Origins and Distribution

With ancient origins in Persia and India, purslane has traveled far and wide, finding its way into gardens, fields, and even urban landscapes across the globe. Its hardy nature and ability to thrive in various conditions have cemented its place in diverse ecosystems, from the Mediterranean to the Americas.

Morphology

Portulaca oleracea is a low-lying succulent plant with thick, paddle-shaped leaves and smooth, reddish-brown stems. In the summer, it boasts small, yellow flowers that open in the morning sun. The entire plant radiates from a central root, sprawling outward in a dense mat.

Nutritional and Medicinal Benefits

Purslane is a nutritional gem, boasting higher levels of omega-3 fatty acids than many fish oils. Additionally, it's a good source of vitamins A, C, E, and essential minerals such as magnesium, calcium, and potassium. Its mucilaginous quality has also been used traditionally to soothe digestive ailments.

Foraging and Harvesting

1. **Leaves and Stems:** Throughout the growing season, especially in the warmer months, the leaves and stems can be harvested. It's best to cut or pinch them, allowing the plant to continue its growth.

Culinary Uses

- **Salads:** The crisp and slightly tangy flavor of purslane makes it a refreshing addition to salads. It pairs well with citrus dressings or creamy concoctions alike.
- **Stews:** In many traditional dishes, purslane is added to stews or soups, where its succulent leaves provide a slight thickening quality and a touch of acidity.

Preparation Tips

- Prior to using purslane, wash it carefully to remove any sand or dirt nestled in its crevices.
- The succulent nature of purslane means it retains water, so it's wise to be moderate with added liquids in cooking.
- It pairs excellently with robust flavors like garlic, tomatoes, and olives, enhancing Mediterranean-style dishes.

Conclusion

Purslane is a testament to the saying, "Don't judge a book by its cover." While some gardeners might be eager to uproot this "weed," those in the know cherish Portulaca oleracea for its culinary and health-giving virtues. It stands as a reminder that sometimes, the most precious treasures are found where we least expect them, and that our very gardens and pathways can be rich sources of gastronomic delight.

Wild Garlic or Ramps (Allium tricoccum)

Lurking beneath the canopy of deciduous forests, especially in the springtime, is a coveted wild delicacy known for its pungent aroma and robust flavor: the wild garlic, or as it's popularly known in North America, ramps. A true harbinger of spring, this plant brings with it both rich culinary traditions and an air of woodland mystery.

Origins and Distribution

Native to the woodlands of eastern North America, from the southern Appalachian Mountains to the forests of Canada, ramps have been a seasonal treat for generations. Their distinctive aroma and flavor have made them sought-after by indigenous peoples, settlers, and modern foragers alike.

Morphology

Allium tricoccum showcases broad, lance-shaped leaves that are a vibrant shade of green. As the season progresses, the plant produces a flower stalk with a cluster of creamy-white flowers.

Below the ground, ramps have small, white bulbs, resembling those of scallions but with a more potent scent.

Nutritional and Medicinal Benefits

Ramps are not only flavorful but also nutritious. They contain a good dose of vitamin C, vitamin A, and selenium. Furthermore, like other members of the Allium family, ramps have compounds that may offer heart and immune system benefits.

Foraging and Harvesting

1. **Leaves:** In early to mid-spring, the leaves are at their most vibrant and are perfect for harvesting.
2. **Bulbs:** While the bulbs are edible, it's crucial to harvest sustainably. Taking only a portion and leaving some to regrow ensures that the population remains healthy and vibrant.

Culinary Uses

- **Salads:** Fresh ramp leaves can be chopped and sprinkled into salads for a bold, garlic-like punch.
- **Sautés:** The leaves and bulbs can be sautéed with other vegetables, imparting a rich, oniony flavor.

- **Flavoring:** Ramps can be used to flavor various dishes, from omelets to risottos, or even turned into pestos and pickles.

Preparation Tips

- Thoroughly rinse ramps before use, especially the bulbs, which can hold onto dirt.
- The potent flavor of ramps can dominate a dish, so use them judiciously, especially when trying them for the first time.
- To store ramps, wrap them in a damp cloth and place them in the refrigerator. They can last up to a week if kept cool and moist.

Conclusion

The allure of ramps lies not only in their unique taste profile but also in their ephemeral nature. Their brief appearance each spring is a celebration of the season's transition. To forage and cook with ramps is to partake in a time-honored tradition, honoring the land's rhythms and the cultural practices that have revered this plant for centuries.

Burdock (Arctium lappa)

Burdock, with its long, tapering roots and distinct burs, is more than meets the eye. While its seed pods might be infamous for clinging to clothes and animal fur, its underground bounty is a treasure in many culinary traditions, celebrated for its earthy taste and health properties.

Origins and Distribution

Originating from the Old World, particularly Europe and Asia, burdock has naturalized in many parts of North America. It thrives in disturbed areas, like roadsides and vacant lots, making it both a recognizable and accessible wild edible for foragers.

Morphology

Arctium lappa is a biennial plant, with rosettes of large, wavy leaves in its first year, followed by tall flower stalks with purplish flowers in its second year. Its most recognizable feature is the bur-like seed pod covered in tiny hooks. But for foragers and chefs, it's the long, brown roots that hold the real intrigue.

Nutritional and Medicinal Benefits

Burdock root is renowned in both traditional medicine and modern nutrition. It's packed with inulin, a type of fiber that supports digestive health. Moreover, the root contains antioxidants and has been associated with detoxifying properties, often used in herbal remedies to purify the blood.

Foraging and Harvesting

1. **Roots:** The best time to harvest burdock roots is during the fall of its first year or the spring of its second year, before the plant bolts. The roots can extend quite deeply, so a sturdy shovel or digging tool is necessary.

Culinary Uses

- **Stews:** Burdock root imparts a sweet, earthy flavor to stews and soups. Its texture, somewhat akin to parsnip, becomes tender and palatable after prolonged cooking.
- **Stir-fries:** In Asian cuisines, especially Japanese (where it's called "gobo"), thinly sliced burdock root is a staple in stir-fries, often paired with carrots and seasoned with soy sauce and sesame.

Preparation Tips

- After harvesting, it's crucial to clean burdock roots thoroughly, scrubbing off any residual soil.
- The outer skin can be tough, so peeling or scraping it off is often recommended.
- If not using immediately, burdock roots can be stored in a cool, dark place for several days, or they can be blanched and frozen for longer storage.

Conclusion

Burdock, a plant so often overlooked or even maligned for its sticky burs, is a lesson in the duality of nature. What might be a nuisance above ground hides a treasure beneath. By delving deep, both into the soil and into culinary traditions, we discover the hidden gems that plants like burdock offer, enriching our meals and our connection to the wild world around us.

Clover (Trifolium spp.)

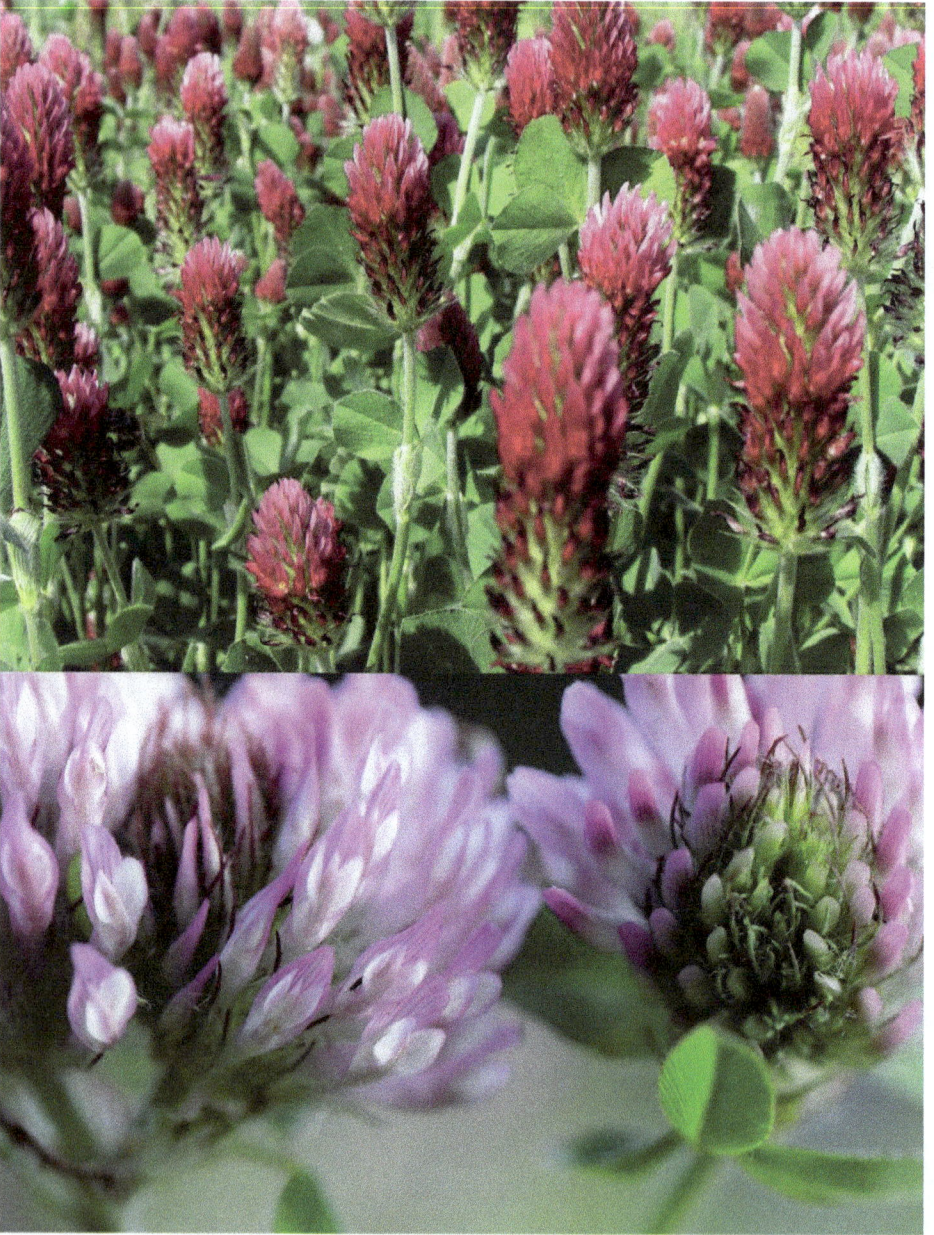

When one thinks of fields and meadows, the image of clover often comes to mind. This seemingly ubiquitous plant, with its trifoliate leaves and delicate flowers, is not just fodder for livestock or a haven for bees. For the discerning forager, clover is a delightful addition to the culinary and medicinal toolkit.

Origins and Distribution

Clover has its roots in the temperate regions of Europe, Asia, and Africa. Today, it has become widespread, found from the verdant pastures of North America to the sprawling grasslands of Australia. It thrives in various habitats, from open fields to gardens, often enhancing the soil with its nitrogen-fixing capabilities.

Morphology

The Trifolium genus is diverse, but most species share some common features. They possess trifoliate leaves, often with a characteristic pale crescent or oval shape on each leaflet. The flowers range from white to deep red, clustering together in pom-pom-like heads.

Nutritional and Medicinal Benefits

Clover is more than just a pretty face in the meadow. It's a source of essential minerals such as calcium, magnesium, and potassium. The flowers, particularly of red clover (Trifolium pratense), have been used in traditional medicine for various ailments, including respiratory issues and skin conditions. They also contain isoflavones, compounds being studied for their potential health benefits.

Foraging and Harvesting

1. **Flowers:** Best picked when in full bloom during late spring to early summer. They should be vibrant in color, indicating peak freshness.
2. **Leaves:** Young leaves are the most tender and can be picked throughout the growing season.

Culinary Uses

- **Teas:** Clover flowers make a mild, sweet tea. Often, red clover is preferred for its richer flavor and medicinal properties.
- **Salads:** Young clover leaves can be mixed into green salads for a subtle, fresh taste, while the flowers add a splash of color and a hint of sweetness.

Preparation Tips

- After foraging, gently rinse clover flowers and leaves to remove any insects or dust.
- For tea, fresh or dried flowers can be used. If drying, spread the flowers in a single layer in a shaded, airy spot until they're completely dry.
- When adding clover to salads, it pairs well with light dressings that don't overpower its subtle flavor.

Conclusion

Clover, often seen blanketing the countryside, holds secrets beyond its pastoral beauty. By bringing it from the field to the plate or teacup, we connect with ancient traditions that recognized the simple yet profound gifts of the land. To forage and consume clover is to partake in a dance as old as time, celebrating the rhythms of the seasons and the bounty of the earth.

Morel Mushrooms (Morchella spp.)

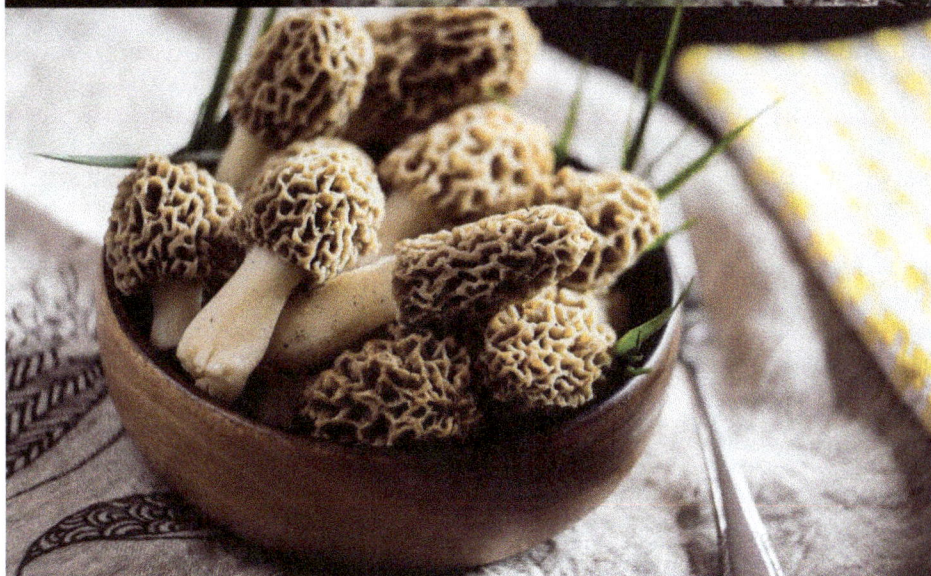

To the avid forager, the arrival of spring heralds the hunt for one of nature's most sought-after delicacies: the morel mushroom. With its distinctive honeycomb appearance and rich, earthy flavor, the morel stands as a true gem in the wild food kingdom.

Origins and Distribution

Morels are native to many temperate regions across the globe, from the hardwood forests of North America to the deciduous stretches of Europe and Asia. Their elusive nature and relatively short season make them all the more prized, prompting annual forays by enthusiasts keen to unearth their hidden treasures.

Morphology

Morchella species are easily recognizable by their unique appearance. The cap is elongated or conical, with a distinct honeycomb or mesh-like surface made up of ridges and pits. The cap connects directly to the stem, creating a singular hollow chamber inside.

Nutritional and Medicinal Benefits

Morels are a good source of vitamins D and B, as well as essential minerals such as iron and copper. They also possess antioxidant properties. However, it's important to note that morels must be cooked before consumption, as they contain hydrazine toxins when raw, which are broken down through cooking.

Foraging and Harvesting

1. **Spotting:** Morels often appear in areas with disturbed soil, such as recently burned forests or floodplains. They also have a fondness for associating with certain trees, like elms, ashes, and apple.
2. **Harvesting:** When you find a morel, cut or pinch it off at ground level to ensure the mycelium below remains undisturbed for future growth.

Culinary Uses

- **Sautéed:** Morels are heavenly when sautéed in butter or olive oil. Their porous structure absorbs flavors beautifully, making them perfect for pairing with garlic, shallots, and herbs.

- **Soups:** Their rich flavor enhances broths and cream-based soups, lending a gourmet touch to any dish.

Preparation Tips

- Before cooking, rinse morels thoroughly in cool water to remove any debris or tiny critters. Due to their honeycomb structure, it's essential to inspect each mushroom carefully.
- Always cook morels thoroughly. Never consume them raw due to potential toxicity.
- Morels pair wonderfully with spring vegetables, wines, and creams. Their distinctive flavor is often the centerpiece of a dish, so simplicity can be key.

Conclusion

The allure of the morel mushroom lies in its fleeting presence, its intricate beauty, and its unparalleled taste. Foraging for morels is as much about the thrill of the hunt as it is about the culinary delights that follow. By understanding and respecting the morel, we delve deeper into the magic of our natural world, cherishing each find as a testament to the wonders of the wild.

Cattail (Typha spp.)

Stretching tall against the backdrop of wetlands, ponds, and lakes, the cattail is a sentinel of freshwater habitats. Recognized by its characteristic cigar-shaped brown flower spike, this plant has been dubbed the "supermarket of the swamp," revealing an array of edible treasures throughout its growth cycle.

Origins and Distribution

Typha species are found across the globe, gracing the edges of freshwater systems in both temperate and tropical regions. Historically, cattails have not only served culinary purposes but have also been vital for their utility in making mats, baskets, and as insulation.

Morphology

Cattails are tall, slender plants, often reaching several feet in height. Their long, linear leaves form dense clumps, while their most identifiable feature is the brown, sausage-like flower head that emerges atop a sturdy stalk.

Nutritional and Medicinal Benefits

Rich in starch and fibers, cattails have sustained humans for generations. The roots, in particular, are a dense source of carbohydrates, while the young shoots provide a dose of vitamins and minerals.

Foraging and Harvesting

1. **Young Shoots:** In the spring, the tender new growth can be plucked from the base. These shoots, with their cucumber-like taste, are excellent when fresh.
2. **Roots:** Typically harvested in late fall to winter, the roots can be dug up, cleaned, and processed to extract their starchy content.
3. **Pollen:** The bright yellow pollen, which appears in early summer, can be collected by shaking the male flower heads into a bag.

Culinary Uses

- **Salads:** Young cattail shoots, crisp and refreshing, can be chopped and added to salads.

- **Flour:** The starchy rhizomes can be processed to make a flour substitute, excellent for pancakes or bread.
- **Soups:** The shoots and parts of the root can be incorporated into soups for a unique, earthy flavor.

Preparation Tips

- Ensure that you're foraging from clean water sources, free from pollutants and contaminants.
- After harvesting, rinse all parts thoroughly to remove any mud or aquatic critters.
- When processing roots for flour, they should be cleaned, boiled, and then mashed to separate the starch. Once dried, this can be ground into a fine powder.

Conclusion

The cattail stands as a testament to nature's bounty, offering sustenance and utility at every turn. By embracing the diverse edible offerings of the Typha species, we connect with ancient practices that honored the wetlands' riches and recognized the cattail as a cornerstone of survival and culinary innovation.

Wild Asparagus (Asparagus officinalis)

Standing proudly against the landscape, the wild asparagus beckons foragers with its delicate, green shoots. A culinary delight and a testament to nature's springtime resurgence, wild asparagus offers a taste that is both unique and reminiscent of its cultivated counterpart.

Origins and Distribution

Native to most of Europe, northern Africa, and western Asia, wild asparagus has been cherished for millennia, both for its taste and its reputed medicinal properties. The plant thrives in sandy and well-drained soils, often found along roadsides, fields, and coastal areas.

Morphology

Asparagus officinalis is a perennial herbaceous plant with tall, feathery fern-like structures that emerge after the edible shoots have matured. In its wild form, the spears are generally thinner than the cultivated varieties and can range from bright green to slightly purplish at the tips.

Nutritional and Medicinal Benefits

Rich in vitamins C, E, K, and B6, as well as folate, iron, and calcium, wild asparagus is not just a treat for the palate but also for the body. Historically, asparagus has been used as a diuretic and is believed to have antioxidant and anti-inflammatory properties.

Foraging and Harvesting

1. **Spotting:** Look for the characteristic tall, feathery growth of mature asparagus to locate patches where the young shoots might emerge in the spring.
2. **Harvesting:** Gently snap or cut the young spears at ground level when they're about 6-10 inches tall.

Culinary Uses

- **Steamed:** A classic preparation, steaming retains the asparagus's crisp texture and natural flavors.
- **Grilled:** When grilled, wild asparagus takes on a smoky, caramelized flavor that's truly irresistible.

- **Sautéed:** Quickly sautéing the shoots in a bit of butter or olive oil with garlic brings out a rich and nuanced taste.

Preparation Tips

- Rinse the harvested shoots thoroughly to remove any dirt or insects.
- Wild asparagus tends to be more fibrous than its cultivated counterpart. If the base is too tough, simply snap it off, and the spear will naturally break where the tender part starts.
- To enhance its flavor, pair with simple ingredients like lemon, garlic, or parmesan.

Conclusion

Foraging for wild asparagus is like joining nature in its celebration of spring. Each spear, tender and full of flavor, tells a story of resilience and the land's cyclical rhythms. Through this journey, foragers and readers alike will experience the joy of discovery and the simple luxury that wild asparagus brings to the table.

Wild Violets (Viola spp.)

Amidst the green expanse of a meadow or the hidden nooks of a garden, the wild violet emerges as a splash of color and a harbinger of spring. With a history steeped in myth and folklore, this humble bloom is not just a feast for the eyes, but also a delightful addition to the forager's table.

Origins and Distribution

Found across temperate regions of the Northern Hemisphere, violets have inspired poets, artists, and healers alike. The genus Viola boasts a vast array of species, with the common characteristic being their heart-shaped leaves and distinctive flowers that range in color from blue and purple to white and yellow.

Morphology

Wild violets are low-growing perennials, typically sporting heart-shaped leaves with serrated edges. The flowers, borne on slender stalks, have five petals: two upward-facing, two lateral, and one downturned, often with delicate veins or patterns.

Nutritional and Medicinal Benefits

Violet leaves are rich in Vitamin C and A, making them a nutritious green to incorporate into dishes. Historically, violets have been used for their anti-inflammatory properties and as remedies for a range of ailments, from coughs to skin conditions.

Foraging and Harvesting

1. **Spotting:** Seek out moist, shaded areas like woodlands, meadows, or along stream banks. The vibrant colors of the flowers make them easy to spot during their blooming season.
2. **Harvesting:** Gently pick the leaves and flowers, ensuring not to uproot the entire plant, thereby allowing it to continue its growth cycle.

Culinary Uses

- **Salads:** The mild, slightly sweet flavor of violet leaves and flowers adds a colorful touch to fresh salads.
- **Garnishes:** The blooms serve as beautiful garnishes for desserts, drinks, or main dishes, adding an elegant flair.

- **Jellies:** The flowers, especially the blue and purple varieties, can be used to make vibrant, floral-tasting jellies.

Preparation Tips

- Wash the leaves and flowers gently under cool water to remove any dirt or tiny insects.
- If using the flowers for jelly, consider combining them with a milder fruit, like apple, to balance the flavors and enhance the violet's delicate essence.
- When garnishing, place the violets just before serving to retain their fresh appearance.

Conclusion

The wild violet is more than just a symbol of springtime's gentle beauty; it's a culinary gem waiting to be discovered. As we delve into the stories, uses, and flavors of the violet, we're reminded of the myriad ways nature intertwines with culture, history, and our very senses.

Elderberries (Sambucus nigra)

Amongst the branches of the elder tree, clusters of deep purple-black berries and delicate cream-colored flowers capture the essence of the changing seasons. With a history that intertwines with folklore, medicine, and culinary traditions, the elderberry stands as a testament to nature's bountiful gifts and its enduring relationship with humanity.

Origins and Distribution

Native to Europe, North Africa, and parts of Asia, the elder tree has long held a place of reverence in various cultures. Its presence in mythology, as a protector or a portal to other realms, mirrors its physical attributes that offer both nourishment and healing.

Morphology

The elder tree or shrub is characterized by its compound leaves, serrated margins, and an arrangement that is typically opposite. In late spring to early summer, it bursts into bloom, presenting clusters of tiny white flowers. By late summer, these give way to the deep, almost black berries.

Nutritional and Medicinal Benefits

Elderberries are packed with vitamins C, A, and B6, as well as iron, potassium, and several antioxidants. They've been traditionally used to boost the immune system, combat colds and flu, and improve heart health. The flowers, too, have their therapeutic benefits, known for their diaphoretic and diuretic properties.

Foraging and Harvesting

1. **Spotting:** The elder tree's distinctive leaves and clusters of berries or flowers make it relatively easy to identify in hedgerows, woodlands, and even urban spaces.
2. **Harvesting:** Snip clusters of ripe berries or flowers using scissors or pruners, ensuring to leave some behind for wildlife and the plant's lifecycle.

Culinary Uses

- **Jams:** The tartness of elderberries makes them perfect for jams, often combined with sweeter fruits or additional sugars.

- **Syrups:** A popular remedy, elderberry syrup can be a daily supplement or drizzled over pancakes and desserts.
- **Wines:** The berries, with their robust flavor, ferment into a delightful wine, cherished by many homemade wine enthusiasts.
- **Fritters:** Elderflowers, dipped in a light batter and fried, are a summertime delicacy in various parts of Europe.

Preparation Tips

- It's vital to note that raw elderberries contain compounds that can be toxic. Always cook them before consumption.
- When preparing elderberries, a simple method to separate them from their stems is to freeze the clusters, then shake or comb the berries off.
- Elderflowers should be used soon after picking and be gently washed or shaken to remove any insects.

Conclusion

The elder tree, with its bounties of berries and flowers, is a symbol of the interconnectedness of life. Its offerings have not only sustained but also healed generations. As we delve into its tales and tastes, the elderberry emerges as a bridge between the ancient wisdom of our ancestors and the modern forager's quest for natural sustenance.

Always ensure that you have the right knowledge and experience to identify edible plants properly. When foraging, it's important to remember the rule: "When in doubt, leave it out." It's always better to be safe and avoid consuming something if you're uncertain about its edibility.

History and Tradition of Edible Herbs

Dive into the verdant realms of history where herbs were the cornerstone of culinary, medicinal, and spiritual practices. As old as civilization itself, the intertwining tales of edible herbs offer insights into our ancestors' relationship with the natural world and its profound influence on cultural narratives.

Origins of Herbalism

The use of herbs dates back to prehistoric times, long before written records. Early humans, through trial and error, would have discovered which plants were safe to eat, which had healing properties, and which were best avoided. Cave paintings, such as those in Lascaux, France, hint at the importance of plants in ancient rituals and diets.

Sacred Texts and Ancient Manuscripts

1. **Ancient Egypt:** The Ebers Papyrus, one of the oldest surviving medical texts, lists over 700 herbal remedies, showcasing herbs like coriander, garlic, and juniper.

2. **Classical Greece:** Thinkers like Hippocrates and Dioscorides penned essential works detailing the use of herbs. Their texts would influence European medicine for centuries.

3. **Ancient China:** Traditional Chinese Medicine's foundations lie in herbalism, with classics like the Shennong Bencaojing enumerating hundreds of herbs and their properties.

Herbs in Mythology and Religion

Herbs often held symbolic meanings and were interwoven into myths and religious practices:

- **Greek Mythology:** Mint has its origins in the tale of Minthe, a nymph transformed into the fragrant herb.
- **Biblical References:** Herbs like hyssop, coriander, and dill are mentioned, reflecting their importance in ancient Judaic traditions.

- **Hindu Practices:** Tulsi or Holy Basil is revered, with temples and households celebrating its spiritual significance.

Medieval Herb Gardens and Apothecaries

During the Middle Ages, monastic gardens became the epicenters of herbal knowledge. Monks and nuns cultivated herbs not just for culinary use but for medicinal purposes. These gardens laid the groundwork for the later establishment of apothecaries and the profession of pharmacy.

Colonization and the Global Exchange of Herbs

The age of exploration and colonization saw the global movement of herbs. Basil, native to India, found its way to Europe, while New World herbs like chili peppers became integral to Asian and African cuisines.

Herbs in Folk Traditions

In various cultures, herbs played pivotal roles in folk practices:

- **European Folk Magic:** Herbs like mugwort, vervain, and sage were considered potent for protection and divination.

- **Native American Traditions:** Herbs like sage, cedar, and sweetgrass were (and still are) essential in rituals and healing practices.

The Revival of Herbalism

In the modern era, as people seek holistic and natural remedies, there's been a resurgence in the interest in herbs. This revival is not just in the context of health but also in gastronomy, with chefs and home cooks alike valuing the nuanced flavors that herbs introduce.

The journey of herbs through time is a testament to humanity's evolving relationship with nature. From sacred rituals to medicinal cures, from aromatic dishes to tales of love and protection, herbs have shaped and been shaped by human history. By understanding this legacy, we don't just honor the past, but we also weave a richer tapestry for the future.

Wild Mushrooms

The mystical realm of fungi presents a treasure trove of flavors, textures, and culinary possibilities. This chapter delves into the mesmerizing world of wild mushrooms, emphasizing the utmost importance of correct identification to ensure safe and rewarding foraging adventures.

Introduction to Fungi: More Than Just Mushrooms

Mushrooms are the fruiting bodies of fungi, a complex kingdom distinct from plants and animals. They play crucial roles in ecosystems, acting as decomposers and forming symbiotic relationships with plants. This understanding deepens our appreciation of the mushrooms we forage and consume.

The Essential Precautions

Foraging wild mushrooms presents inherent risks, as many edible mushrooms have toxic look-alikes. The golden rule is: **If in doubt, leave it out**. Always forage with experts, use multiple field guides, and ensure your finds are double-checked by knowledgeable mycologists.

Key Commonly Foraged Edible Mushrooms

1. **Chanterelles (Cantharellus spp.)**
   - **Identification:** Yellow to orange, trumpet-shaped with wavy edges. Gills are forked and run down the stem.
   - **Culinary Uses:** Sautéed, stews, omelets.

2. **Boletes (Boletus spp.)**
   - **Identification:** Thick stems and caps with a sponge-like underside instead of gills.
   - **Culinary Uses:** Sautéed, dried, soups.

3. **Morel Mushrooms (Morchella spp.)**
   - **Identification:** Honeycomb appearance with mesh-like pits and ridges.
   - **Culinary Uses:** Sautéed, soups, pasta.

4. **Shaggy Mane (Coprinus comatus)**
   - **Identification:** Tall, white, cylindrical cap which turns black and inky with age.
   - **Culinary Uses:** Sautéed when young, before turning inky.

5. **Oyster Mushrooms (Pleurotus ostreatus)**
   - **Identification:** White to gray, oyster or fan-shaped. Grows on trees in shelf-like clusters.

    ◦ **Culinary Uses:** Stir-fries, grilled, soups.

6. **Hen of the Woods (Grifola frondosa)**

    ◦ **Identification:** Large, grayish-brown, with multiple overlapping caps.

    ◦ **Culinary Uses:** Grilled, stir-fried, stews.

7. **Giant Puffball (Calvatia gigantea)**

    ◦ **Identification:** Large, white, round, and smooth. Interior should be uniformly white.

    ◦ **Culinary Uses:** Sliced and grilled, fried.

Tips for Sustainable Foraging

- Only take what you will consume to allow the mushroom to spread its spores and ensure future growth.
- Harvest mature mushrooms, leaving the young to grow.
- Use a mesh bag when collecting, which can help spread spores.

Storing and Cooking Wild Mushrooms

- Store in paper bags in the refrigerator.

- Cooking well is essential; some mushrooms may be indigestible or even toxic when raw.

Foraging for wild mushrooms is a delightful endeavor that connects us to ancient culinary traditions and the rhythms of nature. With respect for the environment, adherence to safety guidelines, and a sense of curiosity, it can be a deeply fulfilling experience that enhances our meals and enriches our connection to the wild.

Wild Medicinal Plants

From the verdant forests to arid deserts, nature offers a bounty of plants with potent medicinal properties. These plants, which have served as the bedrock of traditional healing systems, are a testament to humanity's age-old relationship with the wild. This chapter delves into the rich tapestry of history and knowledge surrounding wild medicinal plants, providing insights into their uses and the cultures that have revered them.

Introduction: Nature's Pharmacy

For millennia, humans have looked to nature for remedies. Before the advent of modern medicine, wild plants served as the primary source of healing agents. Many of today's pharmaceuticals have their roots in these natural remedies, underscoring the importance and potency of wild medicinal plants.

Historical Overview of Medicinal Plants

1. **Ancient Civilizations:** From the Sumerians, who inscribed plant-based remedies on clay tablets, to the Egyptians with their elaborate Ebers Papyrus, ancient cultures extensively documented the medicinal uses of plants.

2. **Ayurveda and Traditional Chinese Medicine:** These ancient systems, dating back thousands of years, have intricate classifications and uses for medicinal plants, many of which are still in use today.

3. **Native American and Indigenous Traditions:** Indigenous tribes worldwide have a deep-rooted knowledge of their local flora, understanding plants not just as medicine for the body, but also for the spirit.

Key Wild Medicinal Plants and Their Uses

1. **Echinacea (Echinacea spp.)**
   - **Historical Uses:** Native American tribes used Echinacea to treat a variety of ailments, especially infections.
   - **Modern Applications:** Often consumed as a supplement or tea to boost the immune system.

2. **Willow Bark (Salix spp.)**
   - **Historical Uses:** Ancient Egyptians and Greeks used willow bark for pain and fever relief.
   - **Modern Applications:** The salicin in willow bark served as the basis for the development of aspirin.

3. **St. John's Wort (Hypericum perforatum)**
   - **Historical Uses:** Used in ancient Greece for various ailments and later in European folk medicine as a remedy for depression and wounds.
   - **Modern Applications:** Commonly taken as a natural treatment for mild to moderate depression.

4. **Ginseng (Panax spp.)**
   - **Historical Uses:** Revered in Traditional Chinese Medicine as a general tonic to enhance vitality.
   - **Modern Applications:** Popular as an adaptogen to help the body adapt to stress.

5. **Yarrow (Achillea millefolium)**
   - **Historical Uses:** Its name references Achilles, who, according to legend, used it to treat wounds.
   - **Modern Applications:** Utilized for its anti-inflammatory properties and to stop bleeding.

Sustainable Harvesting and Conservation Concerns

With rising interest in natural remedies, it's essential to forage and use medicinal plants sustainably. Overharvesting poses a real threat to many species. Ethical guidelines, such as taking only what is needed and promoting the replanting of native species, are vital.

Safety First: Precautions with Medicinal Plants

Many medicinal plants are potent and can have side effects or interact with medications. It's essential to consult with healthcare professionals before using or ingesting wild medicinal plants.

The lineage of wild medicinal plants is interwoven with human history, culture, and well-being. Their stories are a blend of science, tradition, and nature's marvels. By understanding and respecting this legacy, we can bridge the wisdom of the ancients with the needs of the modern world.

Preparing Teas, Balms, and Other Natural Remedies

As the allure of nature's medicine continues to captivate, many find solace in creating their own natural remedies. Harnessing the therapeutic properties of plants in the form of teas, balms, tinctures, and oils allows for personalized healing and a deeper connection to the natural world. This chapter offers a primer on crafting these remedies, ensuring both potency and safety.

Introduction: The Art of Herbal Preparations

From the ceremonial teas of ancient traditions to the healing balms of indigenous cultures, the preparation of plant-based remedies is an age-old practice, intertwining health, spirituality, and nature.

1. Herbal Teas and Infusions: Liquid Wellness

- **Selecting Herbs:** Choosing fresh or dried herbs for specific benefits – calming, invigorating, digestive, etc.
- **Brewing Techniques:** The importance of water temperature, steeping time, and ratios for optimal benefits.

- **Popular Herbal Teas:** Chamomile for relaxation, peppermint for digestion, and elderflower for immune support.

2. Decoctions: Extracting Deep Potency

- **What are Decoctions?** The method of simmering tougher plant materials, like roots and barks, to extract their benefits.
- **Crafting a Decoction:** A step-by-step guide, from selecting materials to straining the finished product.

3. Balms and Salves: Healing Touch

- **The Base:** Understanding carriers like beeswax, shea butter, and cocoa butter.
- **Infusing Oils:** Techniques for infusing oils with herbs, such as calendula for skin health or arnica for bruises.
- **Creating a Balm:** Melting, mixing, and molding your therapeutic balm.

4. Tinctures: Potent Herbal Extracts

- **Understanding Tinctures:** The process of extracting plant properties using alcohol or glycerin.

- **Selecting Herbs:** Choosing plants based on desired therapeutic effects.
- **Making a Tincture:** From herb ratios to maceration times, the art of tincture-making is detailed.

5. Essential Oils and Aromatherapy: Scents and Sensibility

- **Distillation Process:** An overview of how essential oils are extracted from plants.
- **Safety Precautions:** Dilution rates, skin patch tests, and considerations for internal consumption.
- **Popular Oils:** Lavender for relaxation, eucalyptus for respiratory health, and tea tree for its antiseptic properties.

6. Poultices and Compresses: Direct Plant Healing

- **Creating a Poultice:** Techniques for mashing herbs and applying them directly to the skin.
- **Benefits of Compresses:** Using infused waters or oils with cloth for targeted healing.

The Synergy of Nature and Nurture

Embracing the age-old techniques of preparing natural remedies allows us to form a deeper bond with the environment and our own well-being. By understanding the intricacies of each preparation method, we can harness the potent benefits of plants, ensuring that their healing touch remains a cornerstone of holistic health.

Challenges and Solutions in Modern Foraging

In an era where the allure of reconnecting with nature is ever-present, modern foragers face a set of challenges that their ancestors might not have encountered. From pollution to pesticides, these obstacles require knowledge, caution, and innovation. This chapter aims to shed light on these challenges while offering practical solutions for the contemporary forager.

Introduction: The Double-Edged Sword of Progress

As urbanization spreads and industries burgeon, the untouched landscapes ideal for foraging diminish. The pressures of modern life not only encroach upon nature but also leave their marks in the form of pollutants and chemical residues.

1. Pollution: The Invisible Adversary

- **Soil Contaminants:** Heavy metals like lead and mercury can be absorbed by plants. Understanding which plants are hyperaccumulators can help avoid these threats.
- **Airborne Pollutants:** Proximity to industrial areas might lead to plants taking up harmful substances from the air.
- **Water Contamination:** Runoffs from industries and households can lead to water sources being contaminated, affecting the plants that rely on them.

2. Pesticides: A Chemical Quandary

- **Understanding the Risks:** While pesticides are primarily used to ward off pests, their residues can remain on plants and in the soil, posing health risks to humans.
- **Organophosphates and Neonicotinoids:** Delving deep into the most common pesticides, their dangers, and how to identify plants that might be affected by them.
- **Bioaccumulation:** The process through which certain chemicals, including pesticides, become concentrated in

organisms at higher trophic levels, and why it's essential to be aware of this.

3. Solutions for the Modern Forager

- **Strategic Foraging:** Selecting locations distant from industrial areas, major highways, and farmlands that use heavy pesticides.
- **Seasonal Awareness:** Some pollutants and pesticides are more prevalent during particular seasons. Knowing the patterns can aid in safer foraging.
- **Soil Testing:** A proactive approach, testing soils for heavy metals and other contaminants ensures safety.
- **Washing and Preparing:** Effective ways to clean foraged foods to remove potential residues.
- **Community Engagement:** Collaborating with local communities to advocate for reduced pesticide use and better environmental practices can lead to cleaner foraging grounds in the future.

4. Nurturing a Safe Foraging Culture

- **Education and Workshops:** Regular community-based learning sessions can keep foragers updated about the latest challenges and solutions.
- **Digital Tools:** Apps and online platforms can help foragers share real-time data about safe and risky foraging spots.
- **Collaboration with Scientists:** Engaging with environmental scientists and botanists can yield insights into safe foraging practices tailored to specific regions.

Resilience and Adaptation in Foraging

While modern challenges may seem daunting, they offer an opportunity for the foraging community to come together, innovate, and adapt. By staying informed, practicing caution, and nurturing a culture of shared knowledge and community action, foraging can remain a safe and rewarding practice in the modern world.

Foraging Laws and Regulations Across Different Regions

As the popularity of foraging grows, it becomes increasingly essential to understand the legal landscape surrounding this practice. Each region, country, and sometimes even local municipalities, have their own sets of rules and regulations governing the collection of wild plants, fungi, and other natural resources. This chapter aims to provide a comprehensive overview of these laws, ensuring that foragers operate within the bounds of legality and respect for the environment.

Introduction: The Need for Regulation

The surge in foraging's popularity brings with it potential strains on ecosystems. Overharvesting, misidentification, and disruption of habitats can harm the environment. Regulations are in place to prevent such issues and ensure sustainable foraging.

1. North America: A Mosaic of Rules

- **Federal Lands:** National parks, forests, and wildlife refuges have varying regulations. Some permit foraging for personal use, while others have stricter limitations.
- **State and Provincial Regulations:** Each state in the U.S. and province in Canada has its guidelines, often differing widely.
- **Indigenous Rights:** Native American and First Nations territories have specific rules and traditional practices that must be respected.

2. Europe: Ancient Rights and Modern Laws

- **Common Rights in the UK:** From the historic "right to roam" in places like Scotland to newer regulations in England and Wales.
- **Scandinavian Allemansrätten:** The "everyman's right" in countries like Sweden and Finland allows public access to most lands, but with responsibilities.
- **Central and Eastern Europe:** Varied rules across countries, with some nations like Poland having strict foraging regulations.

3. Asia: Tradition Meets Regulation

- **China's Rich Foraging Tradition:** While foraging is historically ingrained, modern regulations vary by region and often focus on specific prized species like ginseng or certain mushrooms.
- **Japan's Satoyama:** The balance between humans and nature in rural areas, and the regulations in place to maintain harmony.
- **Varied Rules in South Asia:** Countries like India and Nepal have specific guidelines, especially concerning protected areas and endangered species.

4. Australia and New Zealand: Protecting Unique Biodiversity

- **Australia's National Parks:** Strict regulations are often in place due to the continent's unique and fragile ecosystems.
- **Maori Traditions and New Zealand Laws:** The integration of indigenous rights and practices with national regulations.

5. Africa: Balancing Conservation with Traditional Practices

- **Protected Areas:** National parks and reserves across the continent have rules to protect biodiversity.
- **Community-based Conservation:** In places like Kenya, community conservancies have their guidelines that work in tandem with traditional practices.

6. South America: Rich Diversity and Conservation Efforts

- **Amazonian Regulations:** With the Amazon rainforest spanning several countries, there are varied rules to protect its vast resources.
- **Andean Traditions:** High-altitude foraging and the associated guidelines in countries like Peru and Bolivia.

The Ethical Forager – Beyond the Law

While knowing and respecting the law is vital, the ethical forager also understands the spirit behind these regulations. Sustainable practices, respect for local communities, and the conscious choice to leave no trace ensures that the world's wild places remain abundant for generations to come.

Preservation and Cooking

Foraging provides a bounty of nature's finest offerings, but the challenge often lies in how to keep these fresh harvests for extended periods and turn them into delectable meals. This chapter will delve into traditional and modern methods of preserving foraged foods, ensuring that the flavors of the wild can be enjoyed year-round. Additionally, we'll explore some culinary techniques to highlight the unique tastes and textures these ingredients bring to the table.

Introduction: From Field to Fork

The joys of foraging extend beyond the hunt; they culminate in the kitchen where wild foods transform into nourishing and delightful dishes. Preserving these ingredients allows us to capture the essence of seasons past, providing sustenance and flavor throughout the year.

1. Preservation Techniques: Keeping Nature's Bounty Fresh

- **Drying:** One of the oldest methods of food preservation, drying removes moisture, preventing bacterial growth. We'll look into sun drying, air drying, and using dehydrators. Best practices for drying herbs, mushrooms, and fruits will be detailed.

- **Salting:** A time-tested method, salting not only preserves but also enhances flavors. Techniques like brining and dry salting will be covered, along with tips for salting greens, seeds, and even certain fungi.

- **Oil-Preservation:** Immersing ingredients in oil creates an anaerobic environment that hinders microbial growth. We'll discuss the best oils for preservation and delve into techniques for preserving herbs, sun-dried tomatoes, and other foraged delights.

2. Cooking with Foraged Foods: A Culinary Adventure

- **Understanding Flavors:** Wild foods offer a spectrum of flavors, often more intense than their cultivated counterparts. We'll explore how to balance and highlight these tastes in dishes.

- **Preparation Techniques:** From blanching nettles to roasting wild roots, understanding the right preparation method is crucial for both flavor and safety.
- **Recipe Ideas:** A selection of recipes will be provided, showcasing the versatility of foraged foods. From nettle pesto to dandelion wine and morel mushroom risotto, there's a world of culinary possibilities to explore.

3. Pairing with Other Ingredients

- **Wild Meets Cultivated:** Suggestions on how to combine foraged foods with everyday ingredients, creating harmonious and delicious meals.
- **Spices and Herbs:** Recommendations on spice and herb pairings to complement the unique flavors of wild foods.

4. Storage and Shelf Life

- **Storing Preserved Foods:** Tips on how to store dried, salted, and oil-preserved foods to maximize their shelf life and maintain quality.

- **Understanding Shelf Life:** A guide on how long preserved foods can be stored and signs of spoilage to look out for.

The Endless Culinary Possibilities of Foraged Foods

Foraging isn't just about the hunt; it's about savoring nature's gifts in the best possible way. With the skills of preservation and cooking, every forager can become a gourmet chef, turning wild finds into culinary masterpieces that celebrate the essence of the wild.

Recipes Featuring Wild Plants

While foraging is a rewarding experience in itself, the true magic happens when these wild ingredients are transformed into mouth-watering dishes. This chapter aims to provide a selection of curated recipes that highlight the unique flavors and textures of various wild plants, ensuring that every foraging trip culminates in a delightful culinary adventure.

Introduction: The Forager's Feast

Each wild plant offers a distinct taste profile, a snapshot of the environment from which it emerged. Through these recipes, we'll explore the diverse culinary applications of foraged plants, from simple salads to complex mains and delightful desserts.

1. Wild Greens Salad with Dandelion and Nettle

- **Ingredients:** Young dandelion leaves, nettle tips (blanched), wild violets, chickweed, wood sorrel, olive oil, lemon juice, honey, salt, and pepper.
- **Method:** Combine greens in a bowl. Mix olive oil, lemon juice, honey, salt, and pepper for the dressing. Drizzle over the greens and toss gently. Garnish with wild violet flowers.

2. Wood Sorrel Lemonade

- **Ingredients:** Handful of wood sorrel leaves, water, sugar, lemon juice.
- **Method:** Brew wood sorrel in hot water until the water turns a light shade of pink. Strain the infusion, add sugar to taste, and a splash of lemon juice. Chill and serve.

3. Wild Garlic Pesto

- **Ingredients:** Wild garlic leaves, pine nuts, olive oil, parmesan cheese, lemon juice, salt.
- **Method:** Blend all ingredients in a food processor until smooth. Adjust seasoning and serve with pasta or crusty bread.

4. Plantain Seed Crackers

- **Ingredients:** Plantain seeds, whole wheat flour, olive oil, sea salt.
- **Method:** Mix flour and seeds, add in olive oil and enough water to form a dough. Roll out thinly, sprinkle with salt, and bake until crisp.

5. Burdock Root Stir-fry

- **Ingredients:** Sliced burdock root, julienned carrots, bell peppers, sesame oil, soy sauce, ginger, garlic.
- **Method:** Sauté ginger and garlic in sesame oil. Add burdock root slices, cook until slightly tender. Add other vegetables and stir-fry until cooked. Drizzle with soy sauce and serve.

6. Elderberry Syrup Pancakes

- **Ingredients:** Pancake batter, elderberry syrup, butter.
- **Method:** Prepare pancakes as usual. Serve hot with a generous drizzle of elderberry syrup and a dollop of butter.

7. Wild Violet Jelly

- **Ingredients:** Wild violet flowers, sugar, lemon juice, pectin.
- **Method:** Brew violets to extract the color and flavor. Add sugar and lemon juice. Stir in pectin and bring to a boil. Pour into jars and seal.

8. Purslane and Tomato Stew

- **Ingredients:** Chopped purslane, diced tomatoes, onion, garlic, vegetable broth, olive oil, salt, and spices.
- **Method:** Sauté onions and garlic in olive oil. Add tomatoes, purslane, and spices. Pour in broth and simmer until purslane is tender.

A Forager's Culinary Journey

These recipes are merely a starting point, a testament to the limitless culinary potential of wild plants. With each foraging expedition, new flavors are discovered, and new recipes are born. The wild offers a continuously evolving menu, ever fresh and always surprising.

The Forager's Responsibility to the Ecosystem

Foraging offers an intimate connection to the land, a way to tap into nature's bounty while exploring the intricate web of life. However, with the privilege of accessing these resources comes the significant responsibility of ensuring the health and continuity of ecosystems. In this chapter, we'll delve into the intrinsic bond between foragers and the environment, emphasizing the duties and obligations that come with every foraging expedition.

Introduction: A Delicate Dance with Nature

While it may seem like a simple act, each foraging decision affects the delicate balance of an ecosystem. As foragers, our responsibility is twofold: to benefit from what nature offers and to ensure its health and vitality.

1. Recognizing Ecosystem Interdependencies

- **A Web of Life:** Every plant has its role, from providing food for wildlife to stabilizing soil. Before harvesting, understand the potential impact on the environment and other species.

- **Rippling Effects:** Removing a plant can impact pollinators, herbivores, and even the soil. Knowledge of these relationships can guide sustainable foraging decisions.

2. The Imperative of Biodiversity

- **Nature's Resilience:** Biodiversity is the backbone of resilient ecosystems. By ensuring diverse plant populations, we help nature withstand stresses like disease or climate variations.
- **Harvest Diversity:** Avoid focusing on a single plant species. Diversify your harvest to lessen the pressure on any one plant population.

3. Non-Invasive Harvesting Techniques

- **Above-Ground vs. Below-Ground:** Harvesting leaves or fruits is less impactful than taking roots. Make informed choices based on the plant's life cycle and the ecosystem's needs.
- **Non-destructive Tools:** Using the right tools, like scissors or pruners, can allow for harvesting without killing the plant.

4. Invasive Species: A Forager's Role

- **Tackling the Invaders:** Some invasive plants are edible and offer a chance for foragers to aid in controlling their spread.

- **Plant Identification:** Crucial to this is the ability to distinguish between native and invasive species. Removing native plants mistakenly can harm the ecosystem.

5. Enhancing Habitats Post-Foraging

- **Seed Dispersal:** After enjoying fruits or nuts, consider dispersing the seeds in suitable areas, assisting in plant propagation.
- **Respecting Habitats:** If you create paths or clear areas for easier foraging, do so minimally, ensuring that habitats for animals or other plants remain undisturbed.

Becoming a Guardian of the Wild

The act of foraging is an age-old dance between humans and nature. By understanding and embracing our responsibility, we transform from mere consumers to guardians. The health and vibrancy of the ecosystem become intertwined with our journey, ensuring a future where both nature and humanity thrive.

Advancing in Foraging

As the world becomes more interconnected, so does the community of foragers. While the act of foraging often starts as an individual journey, advancing in this practice often leads to the discovery of a vibrant, supportive community. This chapter explores the role of foraging groups, the value of community, and how collective knowledge can deepen one's relationship with the wild.

Introduction: The Collective Wisdom of the Wild

Beyond the individual experience, foraging is a communal endeavor. Generations have passed down knowledge, and today, in the age of technology and communication, this knowledge-sharing has taken on a new dimension.

1. The Benefits of Foraging Groups

- **Shared Experience:** Engaging with others provides an opportunity to share tips, locations, and stories, enriching the foraging journey.
- **Safety in Numbers:** Foraging in groups can be safer, especially in unfamiliar terrains or when identifying potentially hazardous plants.
- **Mentorship Opportunities:** Experienced foragers can offer guidance to novices, ensuring knowledge is passed on and traditions are preserved.

2. Local Foraging Communities: Tapping into the Heartbeat of a Region

- **Localized Knowledge:** Local groups often possess a deep understanding of their specific region, from its unique plant life to its seasonal changes.
- **Community Gatherings:** Workshops, potlucks, and group forays can provide both educational opportunities and the chance to connect with like-minded individuals.

3. Online Foraging Communities: The Digital Connection

- **Forums and Groups:** Online platforms like Facebook, Reddit, or specialized foraging websites host communities where members can post identification requests, share recipes, or discuss conservation issues.

- **Apps and Digital Tools:** Modern technology offers apps for plant identification, season tracking, and even community-based mapping of foraging spots.

4. Conservation Efforts within Foraging Communities

- **Joint Initiatives:** Communities can band together to protect endangered species, replant areas, or educate the public about sustainable foraging.
- **Crowdsourced Data:** Collective observations from foragers can be invaluable for scientists and conservationists, offering insights into plant populations, health, and distribution.

5. Cultural Exchange and Global Foraging Communities

- **Foraging Festivals:** Events like mushroom festivals or wild herb fairs can draw international audiences, fostering an exchange of knowledge across cultures.
- **Ethnobotany and Indigenous Knowledge:** Engaging with indigenous communities offers a deeper

understanding of plants, rooted in traditions that span thousands of years.

The Path Forward Together

As the world of foraging expands, the connections we make – both to nature and each other – become invaluable. Embracing the collective wisdom of the foraging community propels the practice into the future, ensuring its sustainability, relevance, and continued growth.

Setting Up an Edible Wild Plant Garden

Cultivating an edible wild plant garden merges the joys of gardening with the delights of foraging. By inviting wild edibles into our backyard or community garden, we foster biodiversity, enjoy fresh foraged meals, and create a haven for pollinators and wildlife. This chapter offers guidance on designing, planting, and caring for an edible wild plant garden.

The Confluence of Gardening and Foraging

A garden of wild edibles serves as a bridge between cultivated spaces and the untamed wilderness. It offers a unique opportunity to engage with nature, learn about native plants, and reap the rewards of a wild harvest right at home.

1. Designing Your Wild Edible Garden

- **Site Selection:** Choose a location considering sunlight, drainage, and soil quality. Wild plants often thrive in conditions conventional garden plants might find challenging.
- **Mimicking Nature:** Aim for a design that imitates natural habitats, like meadows or woodland edges, to ensure plants thrive.
- **Zoning:** Create zones based on plant needs: shade-loving plants, water-loving plants, and those that prefer full sun.

2. Soil Preparation and Mulching

- **Testing Soil:** While many wild plants are adaptable, it's beneficial to test your soil to address any significant deficiencies or imbalances.
- **Organic Matter:** Incorporate compost or other organic matter to improve soil structure.
- **Mulching:** Use natural mulches to suppress weeds, retain moisture, and provide nutrients.

3. Selecting Wild Edible Plants

- **Native vs. Invasive:** Prioritize native plants and avoid those known to be invasive in your area.
- **Seasonal Harvesting:** Choose a mix of plants that offer edibles in different seasons, ensuring a year-round harvest.
- **Beneficial Companions:** Some wild plants can benefit conventional garden plants by attracting beneficial insects or repelling pests.

4. Planting and Caring for Your Garden

- **Planting Techniques:** Wild plants often have unique planting needs. For example, some seeds require stratification (cold treatment) before they'll germinate.

- **Watering:** While many wild plants are drought-tolerant, they'll still benefit from consistent moisture, especially when getting established.

- **Natural Pest Control:** Encourage natural predators, and avoid chemical pesticides, keeping your harvest organic and safe.

5. Harvesting and Enjoying Your Wild Garden

- **Sustainable Harvesting:** Use the same principles as wild foraging, ensuring you never over-harvest and allowing plants to reproduce.

- **Fresh and Preserved Delights:** From fresh salads to jams, syrups, and dried herbs, your garden will provide a plethora of culinary opportunities.

The Living Legacy of a Wild Garden

By creating an edible wild plant garden, you not only ensure a supply of fresh, organic wild edibles but also contribute to local biodiversity, create habitats, and deepen your connection with the rhythms of nature.

The Future of Foraging and Reconnecting with Nature

In our fast-paced digital era, it's easy to lose touch with nature. Yet, the timeless practice of foraging offers a counterbalance, grounding us in the rhythms of the earth. This conclusion reflects on emerging trends in foraging, the innovations shaping its future, and the profound importance of reconnecting with nature in today's society.

Introduction: The Evergreen Appeal of Foraging

Despite technological advancements and urbanization, the allure of foraging remains undiminished. The desire to reconnect with nature, to understand and utilize its bounty, speaks to something deep within the human spirit.

1. Emerging Trends and Innovations in Foraging

- **Digital Foraging:** With the advent of mobile apps, foragers can identify plants, log their finds, and connect with communities, all at their fingertips.
- **Urban Foraging:** As more people gravitate towards cities, urban foraging is on the rise. Public parks, green roofs, and community gardens offer a treasure trove of wild edibles.
- **Foraging Tourism:** 'Forage-to-table' experiences, foraging retreats, and guided wild food walks are becoming popular holiday choices for nature enthusiasts.

2. Challenges and Responsibilities of Modern-Day Foraging

- **Sustainability:** As foraging gains popularity, ensuring sustainable harvesting methods becomes paramount to protect ecosystems.

- **Educating the Next Generation:** Introducing children to foraging not only equips them with valuable skills but fosters a lifelong love for nature.

3. The Importance of Nature in Our Lives

- **Mental Well-being:** Numerous studies point to the therapeutic effects of nature. Whether foraging, gardening, or simply taking a walk, nature offers solace and clarity.
- **Physical Health:** Foraged foods are often rich in nutrients, offering a range of health benefits. Moreover, the act of foraging encourages physical activity.
- **Cultural and Spiritual Connection:** Foraging links us to our ancestors and provides a sense of belonging. Many indigenous cultures regard foraging as a spiritual practice, reminding us of the deeper significance of these simple acts.

4. The Way Forward: Nurturing Our Bond with the Wild

- **Community Initiatives:** Supporting community gardens, local foraging groups, and educational workshops can strengthen the bond between people and nature.

- **Policy and Conservation:** Advocacy for policies that protect wild spaces and promote sustainable foraging is crucial for future generations.

A Timeless Journey

Foraging is more than a hobby; it's a journey of discovery, a communion with nature, and a testament to humanity's enduring bond with the earth. As we move forward, it's our shared responsibility to nurture this connection, ensuring that the wisdom of the wild is preserved, celebrated, and passed on.

www.ingramcontent.com/pod-product-compliance
Lightning Source LLC
Chambersburg PA
CBHW071231020426
42333CB00015B/1429